on Sheep

Diary of a Swedish Shepherd

Axel Lindén

translated into English by Frank Perry

Quercus

First published in hardback in Great Britain in 2018 by
Quercus Editions Ltd

This paperback published in 2019 by

Quercus Editions Ltd
Carmelite House
50 Victoria Embankment
London EC4Y 0DZ

An Hachette UK company

The cost of this translation was defrayed by a subsidy from
the Swedish Arts Council, gratefully acknowledged.

A CIP catalogue record for this book is available
from the British Library

ISBN 978 1 78747 270 9
Ebook ISBN 978 1 78747 271 6

Images © Shutterstock

Excerpt from *H is for Hawk* by Helen MacDonald published by Jonathan Cape.
Reproduced by permission of The Random House Group Ltd. © 2014.

Typeset by CC Book Production
Printed and bound in Great Britain by Clays Ltd, Elcograf S.p.A.

Introduction

It feels rather long ago now, the time we lived in Stockholm. Initially we thought of the move out to the country, to my parents' farm, as a project, as a period when we would be doing something different. Maybe even as a longer kind of holiday. Several of my colleagues at university, where I taught literary studies, had received a grant of some kind to do research abroad a couple of years after completing their doctorates. That sort of thing.

At that time there were several of us who became aware of the environmental crisis and the impending catastrophe. What's going to happen when water fails to come out of taps, electricity from plugs or cash from dispensers? I was also starting to think about global patterns of resource flows. I realised, of course, that the world was unfair, but I hadn't really thought about the direct connection between high and low standards of living. The conclusion I drew, a bit hastily perhaps, was that the only way to seriously tackle the threat to the climate and global injustice, while also making sure of the bare necessities when it all came

1

tumbling down, was to start growing our own food and chopping our own wood. And getting some sheep.

The whole idea was completely absurd in the situation I found myself in back then. I lived in a flat, commuted to work, pretended to be aware by going to political meetings and vegan restaurants. The best thing we could come up with when we used to talk about making a difference was to write an article or start a Facebook group. My colleagues and I might convince ourselves that we barely contributed anything at all to economic growth and consumption. Although this sounded a bit hollow when the salaries we received were spent in full on luxuries and indulgences.

But there was something that appealed even more. A vague and yet powerful feeling. I wanted out. To be outside. In Stockholm, I was like an indoor cat. Everything I needed was in packages, served up in boxes of one kind or another. I was domesticated and made passive, never experiencing any immediate contact with the elements. I never really needed to know what the weather would be like. Suddenly I wanted to be out there, feeling the cold in my fingers, hitting myself on the thumb and wearing my trousers out at the knees.

This feeling was exacerbated by placing the children in a kindergarten on the other side of the inner city. We had to travel by tube for forty minutes every morning and again in the afternoon. The children lay down on their backs along the aisle floor. They were simply exhausted by the situation. It made me think: we don't belong here. We've got to get out.

As if by divine intervention our moving plans coincided with my parents wanting to leave their farm. My parents' farm seemed to be the perfect combination of individual family homes, vegetable gardens, paddocks and agricultural buildings within one commune. At the beginning of the twentieth century the farm had been a kind of miniature feudal society. In addition to the buildings used for agricultural ends a number of homes were built for the people who worked on the farm. With the restructuring of the agricultural sector the feudal lord became just another small businessman, the dwellings were turned into housing for rent and the huge cowshed with the magnificent round barn (a peculiar construction that looks like a combination of Shakespeare's Globe and a pagan cathedral) an abandoned museum object.

The idea was that we would occupy the old core of the farm. The big fields and the cowsheds could be rented out. We took over the tenancies of some of the houses and created an oasis of non-mechanical, small-scale agriculture in the midst of the high-tech, fossil-fuelled landscape of modern farming.

All our friends back in the city, the ones who lived on the same tube line, were convinced we would soon be back. But it was too late. We're sheep farmers and country people now. When I lived in Stockholm my mother used to be appalled by all the noise, the hustle and bustle. It couldn't be good for the children . . . I would roll my eyes, thinking she was a stick-in-the-mud. Now I'm appalled by life in the big city as well. It can't be good for anyone.

One warm evening towards the end of that first summer my wife and I were looking over the hedge at the big fields. We had laboured all day at harvesting root vegetables. We had gathered enough to feed a family for an entire year. From one crop. Huge headlights were sweeping across the fields out there. They were coming towards us. A whooshing and subtly complex sound was getting louder. A gigantic combine harvester swept past us in a disdainful pirouette. We realised that every minute it was gulping down the food supply for thousands of people.

This is the end of the world, I said.

3 July

Baa-ah. So there they are. I can't really see them, but they're usually over in the copse. The sheep. Or a sheep, singular and plural in the same word. I'm thinking about the literary critic Horace Engdahl. A few years ago I used to admire, or I was at least interested in, him and people like him. Someone said Engdahl seemed worried about becoming lonely and insignificant. If you're afraid of being lonely, you've probably never enjoyed true companionship; if you're afraid of being insignificant . . . baah!

5 July

The ewes are all neatly arranged beside the vegetable garden. The group doesn't look that big. There should be twelve ewes plus sixteen lambs, but from this far away it looks more like . . . nine. They seem content. They like lying on a slight slope and looking down. As though they were in control.

10 July

Little tracks are appearing in the paddocks. The sheep step behind one another to avoid wearing down the pasture. It would never have occurred to me to do that.

13 July

It's hot. They are lying in the shade under the broad oaks. They're said not to suffer from the heat despite all that wool. Historically sheep are desert animals. We've got one of those old 'pasture-pumps' in the paddock. The animals can pump water for themselves from a well. There is a kind of lid over the drinking trough and when it gets knocked aside the pump mechanism starts up. The pump is actually intended for cows and only one of the older ewes ever manages to draw up any water, and that's only when she's annoyed. I go over to it and pump up a couple of litres. They really don't drink that much.

1 August

You're supposed to check on the sheep at least once a day. They can manage pretty much on their own in summer, so all you really have to do is make sure they're still alive and that there's water for them. A few of us living on the farm have been trying to share the work of sheep-rearing. We've used various systems for dividing up the responsibilities. People may come and go, but the sheep remain. One of the systems involved noting down the time we spent. A check on the paddock, ten minutes. That seems pretty ridiculous in retrospect. It also took away some of the charm. One of the nice things about having sheep is that every now and then it doesn't feel like a job or a responsibility. A feeling probably best captured in the notion that I'm not the one who has the sheep; it's the sheep that have me.

11 August

I'm doing a round inside the paddock. Everything's okay. One ewe is standing some way away from the others. She looks at me and then looks into the distance and bleats. I have no idea why. She probably doesn't either.

18 August

We keep the group of male lambs separate from the others, because they're starting to become sexually mature and could try to mount the ewes. Sheep puberty appears to have another effect as well – the rams are becoming increasingly intent on escaping. They've been outside the enclosure almost every day in the last few weeks and the problem is actually getting worse. It feels as if they're ready to make a run for it the moment I turn my back. I need to see how they do it for myself. Today I was hovering about close to the flock while trying not to attract attention. It wasn't long before I could see that there were two or three rams behind the initiative to jump over the fence. My off-the-cuff solution was to grab them by the horns and drag them into the round barn. They can mull over their sins there for a couple of days. We keep a bit of extra hay in the barn. As a result the rest of the male lambs have stopped trying to escape, for now at least.

19 August

The sheep were in a good mood today. I started by moving one of the runaway rams from the round barn back into the paddock, to see whether he'd had a change of heart. He bolted on the spot. I carried him back inside and took out one of the others. He stayed with the flock. The two that are still in the barn will probably never stop trying to escape, and we can't waste any of the winter fodder. They'll have to be slaughtered.

20 August

I looked in on the savages in the round barn. They looked back at me defiantly. You're for the chop, is what I thought. They got some hay. Then I checked on the others. There are a lot of thistles in the wooded paddock, the one with the copse in. I enticed the rams outside with some concentrate pellets. They'll learn to follow the bucket soon enough and that will make them easier to move. Then I fiddled about with the little paddock closest to the barn, just running maintenance really, no actual improvements. Like being middle-aged, you have to work harder just to keep up. I opened the gate to the wooded paddock so the ewes could go into both.

23 August

Now the ewes are trying to escape as well. They were outside their enclosure this morning, though it was easy to get them back in at least. They know where they got out, and if you herd them ahead of you they'll return to the hole in the fence. It is as though what they really want is to be home in the paddock but they just can't stop themselves when they see an opening. I felt a pang of self-recognition. Maybe that's just a universal . . . human trait.

24 August

The ewes went good-naturedly back inside today, through a smaller hole this time. I tried to get the electrified wire we set up on the inside of the sheep fence to work in the wooded paddock but it wasn't a very convincing effort. I moved them into Sam's paddock and turned the electricity on. That worked better. The first year we kept sheep a man came to the farm to teach some of us how to shear along with some other minor tricks of the trade. We asked him if the sheep got used to being shorn in the intervals between shearing but he said that sheep have only got three things on their minds: eating, screwing and holes in fences; they take everything else as it comes. All the ewes had discovered the same tiny little hole and all of them went back in the same way.

25 August

Maybe the sheep keep trying to escape because instinct tells them to keep moving from one area of pasture to another. Ideally a flock should be moved between different folds on the land they graze. This makes better use of the grazing because none of the grass has a chance to grow too high. An old saw has it that sheep should only hear the church bells ring in a single Sunday before they are moved on.

28 August

One of the new people on the farm has begun to take an interest in the sheep. This is what she wrote in our messaging-group: 'The leader of the rams ate peas from my hand and snuffled in my face. I don't want to slaughter him; can he be one of the stud rams?' I replied: 'I knew this would happen. You've developed real feelings for them. Just like they do in life, feelings cause problems in sheep-farming. And besides, we can't put the ewes' sons and nephews to stud. The descendants would be cross-eyed and have low IQs. Even lower ones, I mean.' As part of the same conversation she had previously written (which was a bit rich): 'The saga finally came to an end for the savages today. We fortified ourselves with a glass each of blueberry wine and hauled them out of the food cellar and butchered them where the cider-press is. We ended up with two prime fillets, eight steaks, four racks and trimmings for grinding into mince. I cooked one of the fillets for supper. I rubbed garlic and crushed rosemary into the meat ever so tenderly. It was one of the most delicious things I've ever eaten. Almost religious somehow.'

30 August

I've done almost nothing today with the little woolly'uns. I have been thinking about them though. I checked on the water for the ewes. I even went and stood in the middle of the flock to help them stay used to a human presence and to keep the relationship going. Trust is a perishable commodity, in life and in the sheep biz.

31 August

New text message: 'I'm lying here listening to the sheep, they are bleating outside my bedroom. Why do they make that noise? I chose the knives from the catalogue yesterday. I'll put the order in today.' That's love and bloodlust in the same breath.

4 September

Yet another uneventful day with the sheep. You look in on them and start thinking about other stuff. A bit like *Brokeback Mountain*.

5 September

I'm beginning to understand something of the psychology of farming. I don't think about the weather or about the various colours and qualities of the environment, for instance, as something aesthetic. The weather isn't nice or nasty, it's just a practical matter. Cold and clear – check that the water isn't freezing. Windy – make sure the big gate is firmly attached to the wall. Rainy – put something sensible on. The leaves turning – might be time to get the winter feed in. Though there is an inherent beauty in all of this, I suppose.

9 September

The ewes met me today in the farmyard. Nice, if a touch inappropriate. I herded them back inside and repaired the fence.

15 September

I'm ill. If the sheep had tried escaping today, they could easily have run off. Checked the water.

17 September

Strictly speaking I spent the whole day in bed yesterday. My wife said I had to allow myself to recover. But I managed to sneak out and mend some of the fence so the bit between the round barn and the gate is finished. I tried and failed to move the rams, and I gave the ewes some water.

21 September

This virus just won't shift. The rams are refusing to follow the bucket. I don't have the strength to finish the bit of fencing needed before the ewes can go into the round barn. They did get water though. And then there was a hole in the fence around the garden paddock that needed repairing.

22 September

I've got pneumonia. I've only seen the ewes in the distance.
And I'm praying for the rams.

26 September

Back on my feet, more or less. I looked in on the rams this morning. They're fine. The ewes as well. The rams have got a salt lick; the ewes need a new one.

27 September

The grazing is getting poorer. Now is when having a proper system of pasture rotation would be helpful. There would be more for them to eat if I'd managed to move the sheep between the various folds every so often throughout the summer. There is a plan in place. I've split up the paddocks. There are two hectares of grazing land behind the cowshed divided into three different sheepfolds. And then we've got various little paddocks around the garden and in the wooded area towards the road that make up another two hectares. Only there's been no method to the rotation. It's mostly been a matter of finding a particular fold where the fence hasn't got any holes in it at the time. There's a rule of thumb for how much grazing land is needed, five ewes per hectare, something like that. I can't remember exactly, though that figure doesn't strike me as right either. We've got enough for now, that I do know.

1 October

Keeping sheep would be enormously difficult without the use of machinery and fossil fuels. It might not even be possible. Though if (when) the fossil fuel runs out, the sheep will probably manage rather better than the shepherd. I've been trying to get some fence posts to stay in place for a while now. This is in a little stretch that runs across a hard stony patch of land; asphalt was probably laid over it at some point to give tractor wheels better purchase. Needless to say this is the very spot the sheep choose to escape through: where the posts are wobbly. Sinking the posts any deeper than twenty centimetres or so has proved completely impossible, but then today a solution suddenly presented itself. I got the tractor and drove the pallet forks into the earth. The tips left deep holes and the posts slotted into them like concrete.

2 October

I got the fence by the cowshed finished and couldn't help yelling in triumph. Getting it done at last felt fantastic. I hope none of the real farmers heard me. I hope no one heard me. Then again, I hope the ewes heard me. They could do with something to think about. Though they're doing well enough, just trudging along must get a bit tedious. Imagine if all you had to worry about were your most basic needs. Am I hungry? Thirsty? Am I feeling cold? It'd be enough to drive you crazy. Or leave you feeling completely calm.

3 October

I looked in on the rams and wedged open the door to the shed the water trough is in. I moved the ewes to the garden paddock. The gate to the wooded area is open as well. There's a lot of clover along the edge of the meadow; I'm hoping the smaller ewes can fatten themselves up a bit.

10 October

I took a Spaniard with me into the paddock today. He never stopped talking; the ewes looked back at him stony-faced. After that I tightened one of the winches in the slaughter room.

11 October

The shearing this morning went well. It was almost the first time I felt I was fully in control of the process. That feeling has been a long time coming and cost blood, sweat and tears. But it's been worth it. The blood has mostly been shed by the ewes, this year I did hardly any harm at all.

19 October

The ewes are fine. They managed to sneak out for a stroll in the autumn-sown wheat. I left them to their own devices for a bit while I mended the fence. Fresh wheat sprouts are supposed to be good for them. Last year I asked the farmer who tills that field if his harvest was affected by the sheep's repeated escape attempts and their grazing on the tender shoots. 'Not a bit,' he replied with a wry smile.

2 November

The ewes woke up (if they slept at all) to paddocks covered in snow. They were inside the round barn. I'd opened it up yesterday and put down some hay. Most of the winter feed consists of silage that we buy from the real farmers, though we do bring some in ourselves. We scythe the grass and mound it into what might rather generously be called a haystack. Though it's a lot of work for not much fodder, not everything we do in this life can be entirely rational. In any case, being able to give that little tuft of hay to the sheep when the first snow has settled feels rather special. It's like saying, this is what we harvested some months ago and we've been saving it up just for moments like this, when it's snowing and windy and cold outside and the grass in the paddock is all gone. That's not something you could have managed yourselves. I'm really not sure if that is gratitude in the sheep's eyes, it's more likely to be a very basic form of astonishment: Oh right, we were just going to lie down here and die only there's some hay after all.

3 November

I sent a text to the others: 'I had a look at rams today, the Gute breed. Good size, nice colours, horns. I like them. The choice is between Affe and Brolle. Both are pale, a bit streaked. What do you think? Almost time for breeding. Before the end of this week. For the sheep I mean.'

5 November

Brolle it was. He was living with an elderly couple about twenty kilometres away. They've got ten to fifteen ewes. Owners of small flocks have a tendency to give their rams rather over-elaborate names. One owner we bought from named them after celebrated feminists. We did consider the prominent lawyer Claes Borgström but plumped for the Phantom (he defends women, apparently). Brolle's farmers were nice; she showed us photos of her grandchildren, he showed us photos of his sheep. We went through the names of our relatives and friends in exhaustive detail in order to map out all the links that exist between our families. There was something about an aunt on my father's side, which I didn't really get. That's the way it works in the country – like Facebook, only you can never leave. We wrestled Brolle into the boot. Once he was ensconced in the paddock with the ewes, he got the idea straight away. A bit of sniffing and snorting and then wham bang. Can that really be natural?

15 November

I spent quite a bit of time today getting the livestock records in order. They need to be properly up to date as it will soon be time for the tests so we can get our MV-accreditation (a programme that prevents a disease from spreading). It turned out that two of the sheep have the same number: 006. Not that it really matters that much; we can easily tell them apart, one is grey and the other just that bit greyer. Only how could it have happened? I'm willing to believe a lot of them, but not swapping ear-tags.

16 November

Besides our own hay we've got a little patch of meadowland where we grow grass for silage. We don't cultivate it like real farmers; we never compost it, but allow the sheep to graze on it in late summer. For a while I thought the sheep didn't like our silage but today they were chewing away at it intently. They even managed to get into the garden for a while yesterday. One of the posts in the newly renovated section of fence had fallen over. As though the post were determined to yank itself out of the ground. I thumped a stone in beside it in an attempt to wedge it in place. Time will tell. A real farmer would have . . . If only I knew what a real farmer would have done.

18 November

Some people think living in the country is lonely. I've got the sheep though. It's probably not the exact number of encounters you have that determines whether a connection is social or not. It has more to do with the character of the people you meet, and whether you identify with them, whether they want to identify with you and whether you can see yourselves reflected in each other. There isn't that much difference between town and country when it comes to social life. Though here I've got the sheep.

20 November

I'm looking out from the front door. The snow has gone again; there's still a bit of green out there. I realise that even though we didn't really plan it from the start the system we've ended up with here is a good one. The round barn the sheep go into for their winter feed is right next to the biggest paddock. The doors are almost always open so they can make up their own minds when they want more fodder. A neat solution, as I see it; who knows better than the sheep when there's no more grazing to be had in the paddock?

24 November

I turned off the water to one of the summer pastures this morning so the pump wouldn't burst. I've got to remember to do the same by the brook and over by the round barn before the temperature drops even further below zero.

2 December

Sometimes, like today, prising the silage out of the bale is all but impossible. Somehow the tufts of grass manage to weave themselves inextricably together. I keep at it and get sweaty. And angry. We're supposed to work collectively on this farm of ours, that's the whole idea, though clearly it doesn't apply to everyone. I'm the only one doing any work, I think bitterly. I don't get worked up normally but an unexpected rage starts bubbling up inside when I have to labour hard enough to be out of breath. It is cathartic.

12 December

I've had rather less to do with the sheep in the last few days. I go over to the round barn, give the silage a kick or two and look out through the doors. Usually they're out there looking for grazing. They shouldn't be finding any this late in the year but the last tufts of the bale have been slow to disappear. I wonder if the increase in bleating when they see me means they want more food. Though they obviously can't manage all the steps involved: I – want – more – food – give – it – to – me. But an instinct for communicating with humans may have been inherited over the centuries. They're bleating more now. I'm leaving the light on for tonight, so they can go inside when darkness falls and pick at the last bits of silage without a thought in their heads.

13 December

A new bale of silage. The previous one lasted almost three weeks. There was a bit of bother with the tractor beforehand. I had to change the radiator myself. Learning how to do stuff is a good thing, I was thinking. Though I'm bound to have forgotten how the next time the radiator breaks down. When I put out the bale I happened to put a dent in the bars of the stall, which means they'll have to be repaired eventually. Not a huge issue, but it reinforced the sense that we need a new system, better suited to the smaller scale of our operation: small bales for instance. One of my children came with me and got to know Brolle. The sheep have become a bit less tame this last week. Before long it was plain to see that instead of taking the time to walk around the paddock, I've mostly been checking on them from a distance.

16 December

Some new sheep mesh arrived by lorry the other day. I was a bit tempted to repair some of the fences.

17 December

A brief visit to the sheep today. I was pottering about in the round barn and they came trotting in, bleating absent-mindedly. I went over and tugged at the silage so they could get at the bits more easily. They looked at me suspiciously; what I thought was: we have a relationship. They've stopped going into Sam's paddock, though they spend quite a bit of time outside in the wooded one. I wonder if it's just habit that makes them look for grazing, unless they really do prefer frost-nipped blades of grass to silage? One of the sheep seems a bit odd. She keeps moving slowly though she doesn't seem to be in any pain. Depression?

18 December

I spoke to the vet. She said I could wait and see, but that the ewe should be put down if she got a fever and failed to recover. I'm going to take her temperature now.

18 December (in the evening)

Her temperature's only 39.5, which is normal for sheep apparently. She does eat the hay and the concentrate pellets, but other than that she just lies there. I don't really dare believe she's going to survive. We'll just have to see.

20 December

New silage. It went quicker this time. Good technique on the tractor. I banged into the stall bars again though. They creaked a bit but survived. Brolle is usually the first to appear. I don't think he's the leader. He's just the craziest of the lot, the one the others send over when they're feeling insecure. The psychology of rams is interesting, though maybe the way to put it is that the meeting between the ram and the human mind is interesting. When they are on their own in the flock with the ewes, the way Brolle is now, the ram is always the one to come over first and have a nose around; when you drive the flock ahead of you he goes last and stays close to the shepherd and likes to be scratched on his back and under the chin. He's easy to feel close to, to play around with and snuggle up to, and there's no problem getting him to walk alongside you and even come when you call. With a bit of patience a ram can become just like a dog. For a while, that is. There are endless stories about people with small flocks of sheep who feel close to their rams and talk about them as though they were members of the family, only to realise after a while, and with some regret, that they have to be sold or slaughtered. There's always this turning point when the ram can no longer handle the intimacy and has to start butting you. Someone once said this is because rams can't really distinguish between friendship and rivalry; they're the same thing to them somehow. I went through this with our first ram, the Phantom. We used to cuddle like people newly in love until one day he abruptly butted me very hard and deliberately on the thigh. I was given what turned out to be very dated advice that I should wrestle him to the ground, laying him on his back so he knew his place. With the benefit of hindsight it has become obvious, however, that in the long run there are only two existential positions a ram can accept: king of the hill or food for the crows. For several months, though, the Phantom seemed to accept he was my obedient little friend. Then he butted me again. And I wrestled him to the ground again. Three days later and I got another butt. I followed the same procedure and it worked – for half a minute. It was over. We weren't friends any more. I kept away from him. Taking care of the flock became very difficult. I know it sounds horrible but it was a relief when we slaughtered him. And it feels as though someone – evolution, the god of sheep, chance or some other supernatural entity – meant it to be that way. If rams didn't end up being completely unmanageable, we'd never be able to slaughter them and then we wouldn't rear them in the first place.

22 December

The sick ewe appears to be recovering. She's grazing along with the others. Her name is 195. Using numbers might seem a bit impersonal but it feels appropriate nonetheless. Sheep are flock first and foremost and not individuals. We only use real names for the stud rams. Not because we have more respect for them but because for a brief period they have a duty to perform as individuals.

28 December

The shepherd's winter routines have started up again. It's the same every year. The water freezes. I go over with the kettle. I just wasn't able to get the water going today. It was minus twenty degrees and the water had frozen solid in the pipe. I'll have to put out a tubful for them tonight. It may be time soon for a new bale of straw as well.

6 January

A fresh bale of straw in the stall, both for lying on and for eating. I suspect the straw is really just to make them feel full. While I was ripping out some old fencing, I came in for a bit of a lecture from the real farmer, the one who has cows, about all the things to watch out for when harvesting forage. He keeps dairy cows and needs their feed to contain as much energy as possible. Our 'production' takes place during the middle part of the year for the most part, when the lambs are growing, fed solely on natural grazing. Though the ewes are in lamb in the winter, so maybe we ought to keep a closer eye on what we feed them then. All we do at the moment is check they eat their fill. It's a tricky business reading up on what to do because the decisions you have to make depend on whether you want to maximise production or operate as cheaply as possible. There's no one solution, you have to decide for yourself. So we ended up with a new bale of silage. The one before lasted only ten days, but it got the sheep through the worst cold spell even though they had no straw for an appetiser.

8 January

I worked on the fencing yesterday. It isn't really the right time of year; we're in the wrong chapter of the farmer's almanac so to speak. Not that we're really that traditional. The sheep were scared of the roll of sheep netting. They kept looking at it anxiously and tried to move as far away from it as possible. The new silage is completely different, wet and presumably higher in energy. They tuck into it. I mended the saw as well, the one we use to cut points on the posts. It's quite fiddly work. I also connected up the electricity to the small fenced area where we are experimenting with just using an electric wire and not having sheep mesh. It's working perfectly. It was a lot of bother running the connection to the outlet in the white cowshed but it feels like the best solution in the long term.

12 January

Though they're ignoring the straw, they're eating the fodder that is supposedly higher in protein. The snow is settling, which is making work on the fence more difficult. I leant what was left of the roll of netting against the corner of the red cowshed. The stretch across to the greenhouse will be the next project. Parts of a large oak by the crofter's cottage near the woods were blown over. That should make a lot of really good posts.

15 January

Today I managed to check on the condition of some of the ewes with my hands. The all-white mixed breeds are nice and fat; you can barely feel the bone when you press down on their hips. Brolle was a bit thinner and 195 was downright skinny. Not good, but better than being put down and destroyed. I am going to try to do the same check on all of them. They may need supplementary feeding on an individual basis. Doing that was easy when 195 was on her own in the barn while the others were outside, but if I added concentrate pellets now the strongest ones would just eat them all up.

16 January

I checked on a couple more of the ewes. The Helsinge sheep are a bit thinner than the mixed breeds. We've now got proper lighting installed in the round barn. A real boost, for me and for the sheep. I didn't go over there until five p.m. It was dark out and not all of them were inside, I could see only nineteen, there should be twenty-two.

17 January

I felt a few more of the ewes. They were fat, just as they should be.

18 January

A fresh bale. They seemed hungry and were waiting by the rack where the bale is usually kept. I got it in place without any mishaps. Key points: take your time, learn from experience, do the same thing consistently and do it over and over again. Be a farmer, in other words. Or: just do things properly.

26 January

The sheep seem to really like the snow. Although they stay close to the round barn, they're as happy outside as in. I've seen them make their way over to the copse on the odd occasion. They come into the barn when I'm there. I think they try to pick out the best bits of the silage, so when I put down new stuff they all want to be first to get at it. A couple of the ewes are always at the very back of the flock and seem to be the last to get fed. I thought there was room enough for all twenty of them to eat at the same time but it's as though they refuse to let one another through. Five of them can block off almost the entire feeding trough.

1 February

I must have managed to check all of them by feel now. Four or five might be on the skinny side, including 195. I'll do another check in a fortnight; if the situation remains the same we'll have to find a way to help them.

2 February

I wonder how the owners of other kinds of animals go about it. I don't make the same strong ties to individual sheep as, say, a dog owner does; what I feel tied to is the whole business of keeping sheep. I don't make plans or set aside time for getting things done – I just do them. Keeping sheep requires the kind of continual presence that makes it more than a hobby. One way or another I have to tend to them every day all year round and in practice I'm responsible for them round the clock. And even though that is a major commitment, it's not entirely clear what you get in return. Meat? Wool? The reward is more in the commitment itself. You never have to worry about not having a full life, because what is actually filling it is only two hundred metres away in a paddock, chewing the cud, completely – and I mean totally and utterly – oblivious to distinctions of that kind.

6 February

I've got a little treasure trove of old bits of pipe. Even though a real plumber wouldn't give this junk a second look, I find it can usually sort out the problem. I never have exactly the right part I need; instead I have to make the best of what I've got. The water trough for the sheep has started leaking, which means a union fitting has to be replaced. I haven't got any of those, so I'm forced to use an oddly bent piece of pipe that looks as if it once belonged in a restaurant kitchen. It works fine.

9 February

I've been reading about climate change and the deterio-
rating prospects for life on Earth. What if this is really the
end? Maybe the sheep worry about that too. As I see it, a life
with sheep is sustainable. In former times all people needed
were sheep. They could be turned into food, warmth,
clothes, toys. Now we buy almost everything from China.

11 February

I haven't had that much to do with the sheep; I've been brooding quite a bit instead. Last year I kept them shut in the round barn throughout the last few weeks of winter so as not to wear down the grass until it was ready for grazing. Housing the flock, they call that. This year I am not so sure.

16 February

I checked on their state of health again this Saturday. Four of the thinner ones have actually put on weight. Only 195 was as thin as a rake. Their recovery could be down to several factors. Might be the silage bales and the fact that there has been more protein in the most recent two, or the way I've been distributing the feed better and putting a tuft or two in the middle of the stall every day. So no one has to stay at the back waiting for their chance to eat.

17 February

I was working underneath the barn roof for a while, which meant I could look at the flock from above. They were shoving against each other at the feed trough. Brolle butted one of the ewes. They are so easy to deal with. I don't need to worry about how well we get on or what really drives them. They don't need performance reviews or pep talks. They do almost nothing in any case, unless ruminating can be considered an occupation.

2 March

They're eating a lot all of a sudden. The kids were playing with them for a while. The sheep made two escape attempts yesterday. Though 'escape' makes the attempts sound rather more animated than they actually were. They just stood there staring and didn't seem to have any direction in mind. The first time a border collie herded them back in without having to be told to do so. It just did it, without apparently worrying the least bit about what the point was. The second time I was the one to do the herding, dithering, anxious, where did they get out? The fence will have to be mended . . .

5 March

I've been thinking about the life I share with the sheep. In one sense it doesn't amount to much. We stare at one another for a few minutes a day. But looking after living creatures is about more than relating to individuals. They are in my care, a state of affairs that is only partially apparent in the mutual staring. Most of the looking after takes place without the presence of those being looked after – the fencing, the winter fodder, the mucking out, the watering. Sheep are said to have been domesticated for 11,000 years. We look at one another, the sheep and me, and it feels like staring into a deep well of experience: problems and possibilities, sources of sorrow and happiness – life in all its dimensions and its inconceivably vast expanse across time and space.

10 March

Their hooves need trimming. There's quite a bit of literature on the subject. I say that without exaggeration. There
is any amount of information to be had in books and on
the internet about how to cut the nails of sheep. Hoofcare
is, however, an excellent example of what some academics
refer to as tacit knowledge (dissertations have even been
written about the subject). I'm not really sure why this form
of knowledge is tacit; maybe it's just modest instead. If you
know how you just do it, if you don't you remain clueless.
Cutting off the outer parts of the sheep's hooves is not difficult. The fact that it may be a bit hard to explain exactly
how to do it is bound to be because you have to be holding
a real hoof to learn the knack. All these books, sites and
dissertations are instances of neurotic compensation on a
huge scale for the lack of physical contact. Another key to
knowledge is making mistakes. I think I've erred on both
sides of the hoof-cutting debate. On the one hand, there's
the option of not cutting them at all. Later on that same
summer I watched as a couple of ewes started hobbling.

Their hooves were seriously overgrown. Not very pleasant but now I know exactly why they have to be trimmed. The other mistake is to cut too much. Half a hoof-pad got lopped off on one occasion. The poor sheep hobbled and bled but was okay in the end, and now I know precisely where to draw the line between the hoof and its pad.

10 April

A couple of the mums – we call them 'mums' when they've just had lambs – keep shoving their lambs away so they can't get at the teat. We have to hold these mums still a couple of times a day. I was absolutely furious with them at first but now I've come to terms with the fact that they're just being sheep. You can't identify with these animals. They are utterly unlike us.

12 April

I'm in the paddock, watching and waiting. One of the
ewes has just had lambs. We've decided to let them do the
lambing outside, so they can choose a spot of their own. It
can get crowded inside the hay barn and it isn't hygienic.
They manage the whole process entirely by themselves.
Some lambs die, that's nature's way, but so far none of the
ewes has had a problem with actually giving birth. She is
licking one of the lambs attentively, the other one is on
the ground a little way off. (Our sheep almost always have
two lambs.) This is a critical moment, or so I imagine: it
may be when she decides to reject one of the two. In a
little while I'll place the lambs inside a separate stall in the
barn where the straw is clean and the space confined, so
the lambs don't have to go far to find the ewe. But I don't
want to pick them up too soon, in case the ewe gets the
idea that the lambs aren't hers. You have to be present but
you shouldn't interfere.

15 April

The children may not be particularly interested in winter feeding and the seasonal routines, but when the lambs arrive they perk up. There is a lot of noise and excitement about who gets to bottle-feed the puny ones and what they are going to be called. Those names don't last long. By the end of summer they won't look like lambs any more. They'll have turned into sheep. The rams will be slaughtered; some of the ewes will be allowed to survive to increase the flock. By then the children will have forgotten both the names and the sheep. That's just the way things are.

17 April

We tried out a slightly unusual method for getting a ewe to accept a rejected lamb. She was allowing one of them to suckle but kept shoving the other one away. So we shut the ewe into an enclosed space and lifted the lamb she liked out of the pen. With the first one gone she might just accept the second lamb. Only then people started feeling sorry for the first lamb. I brought it into the house. My daughter put a nappy on it and took it to bed with her. Though that looked rather sweet, superficially at least, it must have been a nightmare for the lamb. An hour later and I was carrying it back.

7 May

The lambing did not go well. Almost every third lamb was far too puny when it was born, some of them died. It has been awful. It could be down to a virus, the result of one of the silage bales being bad, or – horrible thought – because they weren't fed enough mineral pellets. It would be my fault in that case, and not bad luck, not nature's course, my fault pure and simple. The lambing period lasts for about a month; now that it is reaching its end I am beginning to come out of some kind of stress-related depression. It wasn't just the sadness, the grief even, over lambs dying; a lot of the lambs needed bottle-feeding and help getting to their mothers and all of that was hard work.

16 May

We've had a minor cold snap. Last night it was just a few degrees above freezing and it rained. I went out at midnight. There's only one lamb left that still needs supplementary feeding. I moved into the flock with my headlamp on, they feel safe around me and just stood there staring. Where was the little one? Not with its mum, I could make out the numbered tag in her ear. I walked round the entire flock, no tiny white lamb. Worried. I was humming a pop song, the silly words about love began to be about the lamb and me. Where are you? I need you. I never knew I would miss you this much. Can we turn back time? Time is a river. Hold back the river let me look in your eyes, hold back the river so I can stop for a minute and be by your side. And there it is on the ground. With blood coming from its throat. One of the flying scavengers must already have been at it.

1 June

It's as if the sheep are defined by the flock. What individual characteristics they have are determined solely by the role they play in the group. It is almost always the same individual that finds holes in the fencing, for example. Some sheep are more inclined to defend themselves and the flock, while others keep to the very middle, completely shielded by the rest. I also think they play slightly different roles when it comes to looking for grass; some appear to get sent off from the group to scout further afield. It's almost as though you could see the flock as a single being and its members as different aspects of the same organism. What if the sheep see us humans the same way?

14 June

I meet more people than I need to or that I care to, it can border on hectic at times. Which is why the times with the sheep, particularly when I am with them on my own, become oases of stillness, contemplation and dignity. Even when I have to rush round and get the flock to jump back over a fence or wrestle with a large ram so I can shear his wool, there's a sublime sense of peace to my existence. I think this has to do with my being in direct relationship with something that is alive and yet almost uncompromising in the way it moves. The behaviour and habits of sheep – handed down through countless generations – the grass growing, the rain, drought, cold, heat, food, poo – all of it goes on its merry way without any regard for what I think. The shepherd may be alone but he always has company.

4 July

We had a Facebook page for a while, to prove we actually exist and to show people what we do on the farm. We grow our own vegetables, chop wood, keep a few animals and are trying, without overdoing it or taking the whole thing too seriously (moderation is a virtue), to develop a sustainable way of living. As the representative for sheep-rearing, or maybe even for the sheep themselves, I posted the following brief note: 'The sheep do not graze on all the grass to be found in the paddocks, they choose certain blades of grass and leave others. They do not gorge indiscriminately. This helps the grass bounce back. In the long term, over several years perhaps, the grazing improves and so as a result do the lives of the sheep. Thanks to their restraint. An animal species that constantly satisfies short-term needs without regard to anything else is bound to fail.' Below the text was a photo of how the landscape is being changed by oil extraction in Canada. A green and rolling wooded landscape of lakes and meadows is being transformed into a black gravel desert. I thought it was an accurate and particularly striking little reflection on my part. However, it got very few likes and no comments at all. Social media are said to provide people with attention and affirmation. That obviously doesn't apply to me or the sheep, as long as we're not lying on a grassy slope in the morning mist that is, chewing the cud and pretending nothing is happening, that nothing has anything at all to do with anything else. It may be you have to toe the line if you want approval, but just what kind of love is that?

8 August

One of the ewes is limping. Sometimes this will just be a pebble that has got stuck between their toes. I get hold of her and take a look. I can't find anything, no pebble, no swelling. I ring the vet. It's the same old: wait and see or put her down. Only it's got to be tough limping along on one leg, hasn't it? They've got four of them, the vet replies.

20 August

Someone asked me what sheep smell like. I don't really know, never thought about it. That will be up to the beholder's . . . nose. The ewes have a gland right next to their teats. It looks like a suppurating wound, which makes finding out what it smells like pretty off-putting. The gland helps guide the newborn lamb, presumably by scent alone. My family often say I smell of sheep when I've been shearing them. I think the smell is like that of a well-worn sweater, still bearable, but in need of a wash.

1 September

I'm walking behind the flock. They're almost trotting along ahead of me. Whatever happened to the one who was limping? I can't even remember what her name was. I start urging the flock on a bit faster in order to make sure none has got a problem. The ones with ailments always end up falling behind. Not an infallible system, but it will have to do.

17 October

I bolted the gates on before the slaughter. That didn't go well; I made a mess of it and smashed a bolt. I'll have to buy a new one. That's not going to stop me though.

19 October

You really can't describe the slaughter. Maybe because it is revolting, maybe because the boundary between life and death is just not meant to be apprehended. Either you're alive or you aren't. In between is a vacuum, nothingness, anti-matter. It is like one of the rides at the funfair in Stockholm – the Giant Drop. Your entire body is screaming no, every instinct inside you is resisting for all it is worth but you've made up your mind. This has to be done. And it turns out okay. Only there's no sense of euphoria or relief afterwards. Just this dark grey feeling of completion. No year with the sheep is complete until the slaughter comes round; life with the sheep cannot come full circle until it has been done.

21 October

I mended the fence yesterday from the paddock to the slaughter room. That took an hour and a half in actual time. But it felt like it took all day.

22 October

I've managed to find a bolt gun. The man who lived in one of the houses on the farm before we arrived had one. You can have it, he said, I never use it. I asked him what size it was. Oh no, he replied, you can't use it on mice. The batteries in his hearing aid must have run out again.

24 October

A few thoughts the day after the slaughter. This is the first year we've managed everything ourselves. We used to get a specialist in, a nice man who had been in the meat production business for fifteen years but is currently working in psychiatric care, I believe. So we were able to look away or pretend we weren't really there. But this time we were right in the thick of it. There was a lot of blood and death, and you don't get inured to it. Twelve dead sheep are twelve dead sheep. Twelve shots of the bolt gun mean twelve crushed brains. It's that simple. There is an old tradition that you have a wee dram before the slaughter. As I realise now, that's not because it is fun.

30 October

I'm having a look at the skins. We salted them right after the slaughter. After a week or so you're supposed to check whether they need more salt. The fat must not be allowed to turn rancid. The real slaughterman was very good at removing the skins; it's a tricky stage in the business. You can easily make holes by accident. I can't really see whether we've done it right or not. That'll become evident when they arrive at the tannery.

18 November

I can't stop thinking about what I am doing. And then having another think before starting all over again. Ruminating, you might say. On this business of writing about what my day with the sheep was like, say. How should it sound? A fairly large part of the work is solitary and fairly boring, grey and uneventful. So shouldn't my notes about it be a bit dull as well?

22 November

I did a check on the sheep; wet, cold, windy.

22 November (evening)

I tightened up a fitting to the water supply; the pipe was leaking; cold . . . wet.

23 November

I'm scooping up silage; it's wet, heavy.

24 November

I checked on the sheep; nothing's changed.

25 November

Silage; wet.

26 November

I did a check on them; couldn't see anything.

27 November

Is number 264 limping?

28 November

No.

29 November

Is she?

5 January

I'm having a browse through my notes. What strikes me is the way life here has turned out to be completely different than I was expecting. The fact that I should feel such strong ties, not just to the sheep, but to the grazing land, the changeableness of the weather, the character of the different seasons, the grass, the trees, the bushes, the barns, the fences, the planks, the nails, all of it – is not something I'd ever have believed. When we moved here it was with notions of being part of a commune, of being self-reliant and living a sustainable lifestyle, that kind of thing. It didn't really turn out that way, particularly the commune side of things. (To think, the sceptics always end up being right!) I've had to spend long periods on my own with the sheep. I used to get angry, not so much at the people who weren't there, but at the fact that normal life could exert such a powerful attraction. Having a job, being able to take off whenever you want, doing the conventional thing – turned out to be easier than looking after the sheep. And I can understand that, it isn't as though our very lives depend on sheep-rearing exactly. On the face of it there's nothing to justify becoming a small (unprofitable, that is) sheep farmer and, even so, the sheep demand quite a bit of work on your part. Animals can't just wait around until you feel like looking after them, as my aunt once pointed out to me. So now I've learnt to stop trying to get other people motivated and not let whatever hopes and ideas they have bother me. I take care of the sheep and I'm content with my lot. We've been through disappointment together, the sheep and I. That creates a bond. Not to them as individuals – sooner or later they'll be slaughtered come what may – but to the flock and its needs. I'm not angry with anyone any more.

15 February

I've started reading books again. I'm not sure why. Maybe because the sheep have stopped trying to escape. Though the real difference is bound to be because the electric fence is working better. The winter routines are running much more smoothly as well. The water almost never freezes. There was a time I kept having to repair the system – an electric cable runs inside the pipe to keep it heated – only now it seems to operate without fail. Just think if there were a final repair, one that would last for ever. Even the feed racks have stopped breaking. I'm not complaining about these changes, mind you, it's just that now I find myself indoors looking at the bookshelves. Books tended to fade into the background for most of those first years on the farm. They became furniture, like a tasteful break in the pattern of the wallpaper. I quickly find my way back onto well-beaten paths. Roland Barthes in his *Critical Essays* wrote about the importance of variety and originality in literature. I think he writes something like a message has to be invented to be correct. It occurs to me that it may apply to everything and that for something to be authentically real, you have to avoid routine, experience, even knowledge. When you get too good at doing something, it stops being fun. Telling the same joke twice in a row is really tricky. I hope the sheep will retain their inscrutability. They might even outwit the electricity.

10 March

You become increasingly sensitive to details and signs as a sheep farmer. With the advent of spring and the shift from winter fodder to grazing you need to get a feel for whether the sheep are hungry and if enough grass has grown for them or you need to put out a new bale of silage. It sounds so simple once you've got the hang of it, only it has taken me several years to reach that point. Now when I move into the flock I can tell how hungry they are by how much they bleat and if they are trying to get to me. Sometimes they'll even go over to the gate that leads to the next paddock on the rotation list. Though it may not just be about my being able to read the signals, the sheep may have learnt to give these signals to me as well. We've got each other, the sheep and me.

3 April

The grass, hay and silage are not just what they eat; the sheep really live with them as well. The straw catches in their wool; they get grass stains on their knees. If I didn't know better I could easily imagine them absorbing the plant fibres through their ears, their eyes and even through their skin.

12 April

I saw an advert for some association or other for Swedish farmers. It showed a man looking over his fields, his rather large, flat and well-ploughed fields, as the sun is rising. He gets up on his tractor, looking like a passenger on a double-decker bus. The voiceover tells us that the farmer lives off the land and that's why he cares about it. I don't think I could conceive of anything more screwed-up, not in my wildest dreams. If you know even the slightest thing about how ecosystems operate then you know that intensive farming is nothing less than a campaign of extermination against large numbers of animal and plant species. It is also systematically depleting the soil – in the long term nothing will be able to grow without the addition of artificial fertiliser – and it guzzles energy to a truly monstrous extent. Sweden's farmers may be hard-working and good at what they do but that does not include caring for the environment. And all the same we and our sheep depend on farmers with big tractors for so much. I dream, though I admit to being torn, about bringing in the feed for the winter by hand, or possibly by horse. Which would need fodder of its own.

21 April

I'd like to think we're becoming more professional with each passing year (whatever that's worth). For one thing, we've got one sheepdog and sometimes two these days. Many of the operations that used to risk descending into farce – such as dividing a group into two flocks and moving one of them to a new grazing ground – now get done without a hitch. Chaos, however, reigned all over again today. We were supposed to move on the ewes and their lambs to a paddock they had never been in before. Ewes with lambs have an entirely different psychological make-up to ordinary sheep. It is as if their instinct to flee has completely abandoned them, along with any urge to keep the flock together. They are entirely focused on the lambs. They wouldn't back away from the sheepdog; some of them even went on the attack. It wasn't long before we had to put the dog back on the trailer. We tried enticing them along with concentrate pellets. That didn't work either. We ended up more or less having to shove them ahead of us.

22 April

I think the fox has taken one of the lambs. The paddock we moved the sheep to yesterday is some way away from the farm, towards the edge of the forest. One of the lambs still needed bottle-feeding and had been partially rejected by its mother. It failed to turn up when we arrived in the morning with the bottle, it was just gone. I talked to one of the neighbours, a hunting fanatic. He told me the fox might take ten to fifteen lambs over the spring; that they have huge problems in England; that the fox has to be hunted down mercilessly and that he has a mate with a terrier that could 'clean out' the den. I brought our conversation to an end. But I couldn't help sneaking up to the edge of the woods and lying in wait with the rifle. I've never shot a fox of any kind; I had one in my sights once but hesitated for too long. Hunting's not my thing. I remained on watch in the grass for an hour until it was pitch black. Then I made my way over to the sheep. They had adopted battle formation. Eighteen ewes and thirty-seven lambs were pressed together in a space no more than twenty-five square metres, the ewes on the outside and the lambs in the centre. They'll be fine, I'm sure.

30 April

I have lost being in daily contact with the sheep. There are some newcomers to the farm who want to be involved. Someone else has been checking on them the last few days, counting the lambs, seeing how much they've been growing, watching what they're grazing on, the stones they jump onto and getting a sense of the mood in the group. There's a feeling of emptiness. It's easy to think being tied down to your responsibilities for the animals is a burden, that feeling you have to be on hand every day is a source of stress, and that you're not entirely free. In fact, it's exactly the other way round. I'm sitting in the kitchen staring into space. There's nothing free about that.

2 May

I'm not vain, but whenever I've done the sheep-shearing before it was as if what I wanted was people to see me. There's so much talking and planning every time the shearing comes round. There are the wool ladies who are supposed to turn up, the neighbours who want to watch, the children who are keen 'to help'. It feels like a small funfair is paying us a visit. And it's not as if I'm even that good at shearing. This time I went over to the round barn and just got started, no one else was around on the farm, and all of a sudden I understood the real meaning of sheep-shearing. I only understood it in vague terms, though I definitely got it, without any words. The wool was greasy and scratched.

3 May

The fact that the world is unsustainable is constantly making itself felt. Or not exactly felt . . . Everything simply is unsustainable, all the time. I don't really understand why everyone acts as though nothing is happening, as though there were any major ideas being put into practice that could make a difference. I've been taking a bit of an interest in forestry since I inherited a plot of woodland (there's a reason for everything). Logging is one of the things helping to bring human life on Earth to an end. It's not really something you're actively aware of; it's more like a net whose threads get snapped one by one until suddenly the whole thing falls apart. Sooner or later the use of clear-felling as part of forest management is going to weaken the connections at work in our ecology to the point where they will no longer be capable of binding the whole environment together. Commendably, the Swedish Forestry Agency has been investing some of its resources in developing forms of forest management that avoid clear-felling. When you talk to the officials at the Agency they give you the impression that opposition to clear-felling is trendy at the moment, it's the current thing and a lot of people are taking an interest. I asked how large an area would actually be re-zoned. At most it is a fraction of one per cent of cultivated woodland as a whole.

9 May

We're fencing in a whole new paddock. Though a paddock is what it has been for several hundred years, just one with barbed wire and cows. We are switching to electric fencing, which will allow the sheep to graze the area along with the cows. The cows belong to the real farmers who rent the land and the cowsheds here. They, the farmers that is, have been uniformly positive to our alternative approach. When we moved here I was expecting more opposition. They must realise, I suppose, that we're never going to take over.

11 May

I wasn't born a farmer, but I'm becoming one. Not a farmer in the sense of someone who works the land, nor an agricultural producer or a businessman. I am becoming a farmer as in someone who is blinkered, unsociable and knows best. I've got the sheep and I don't need anything else. As for whatever else is going on . . . by the way, what is going on?

13 May

More animals are arriving on the farm. Pigs – fun, sociable, basic, much like us humans (apart from sour milk being their favourite food); horses – strong, loyal, useful, not at all like us humans (apart from a latent tendency to go stark staring mad). But the sheep still feel special. There's something quiet and unpretentious and stoical about them that appeals to me. I do another round of the paddock. I really ought to check the voltage in the electric fence but I come to a standstill in the midst of the flock and forget all about it. I slouch home in the dark, reluctantly, as though in my heart of hearts I wanted to stay out there.

16 May

They can manage almost entirely on their own now. I don't have to devote any working hours to them at all, as long as the fence remains intact, that is. Spring and summer (and autumn to some extent as well) used to mean continually hunting for holes in the fence, for the sheep just as much as for me. That's all under better control now. They show great respect for the electric fence, maybe because they don't really understand electricity, but then who does?

23 May

I like to count the lambs every day but it's not that easy. They spread out and move around, particularly when I head towards them. Some of them run off, others come over. There was this thing on television many years ago. It was about sheep-counting in Australia. There were thousands of them that had to be counted. I didn't have much insight at the time about what I was watching but now I understand how they did it. The flock was herded towards a gate that only allowed two sheep to pass through at any one time. With the flock crowding in on them from behind, the animals flowed through the gate at just the right pace for the man who was doing the counting. Something similar happened here the other day – quite spontaneously. If one of the gates is left open, the sheep will happily move on to a new paddock. I opened it a tiny bit and realised that if I held it open at just the right angle the sheep would run across at the perfect speed for me to count them: thirty-seven lambs.

5 June

I realise what I am about to write is a bit of a cliché. It isn't particularly accurate either, but it's an idea that keeps cropping up when I'm having a think. Perhaps my relationship to the sheep mirrors something in my past; it may be a lost childhood I can see in those vacant eyes. This proximity to the semi-civilised, semi-natural world could be exactly what I've been missing. I grew up in these parts. My father used to run this farm. My tender childish feet trod on the ancestors of these very nettles. And that experience may live on at some very deep level in the soles of my feet. There was this thing I could feel as a child, a sense of there being connections that cannot be identified but which feel real to the person who is . . . open. Subsequently I was taught that the opposite is true. The world is put together in a logical way; you approach it through education and by improving your command of the subjects that science or knowledge dictates. That other stuff is mostly treated as a joke. During the first half of my life my own development was more or less a copy of industrialism itself: rational, progressive, urban. The sheep are making me barefoot again, so to speak. A return to the simple things. Only what is simple turns out to be extremely complex, with many different facets.

11 June

I'm reading *H is for Hawk* by Helen Macdonald. She tames a goshawk as a way of working through her grief at her father's death. And coming to terms as well perhaps with the pointlessness of her self-image as an academic. I don't really understand at first that this is about acquiring a piece of hunting equipment. It's so hard to believe that a raptor can retain all its instinctual skills as a wild animal and still remain faithful to its owner. I knew that this had been the case historically, but it's as if my involvement with the animals on the farm has made the idea of tame birds of prey completely improbable. In any case, she describes a trip to look for goshawks and how she gets out of her car like a deer coming out of hiding. 'Something inside me ordered me how and where to step without me knowing much about it. [. . .] Those old ghostly intuitions that have tied sinew and soul together for millennia had taken over, were doing their thing, making me feel uncomfortable in bright sunlight, uneasy on the wrong side of a ridge, somehow required to walk over the back of a bleached rise of grasses to get to something on the other side: which turned out to be a pond.' I know what she means. There's something between the sheep and me that is much older than either of us, older than these bushes and trees, older than books and knowledge. The bird is supposed to learn to hop from its perch to the owner's gloved hand. It's not really working. The hawk stays on its perch, sulking. But then something happens. 'My hand is hit, hard, with a blow so unexpectedly powerful the shock is carried down my spine to the tips of my toes. Hitting someone's hand with a baseball bat would have had a similar effect. [. . .] She has crossed a great psychological gulf, one far wider than the ten inches between her perch and the glove she's landed upon. Not that she's landed on it: she's killed it.' This may be overstating it a bit but I understand that seductive sensation of being in direct contact with the natural world. I'm thinking of the lamb getting a proper hold on the teat for the first time. That tiny little body, barely capable of keeping itself upright let alone finding its way around. But when its mouth suddenly gets a good grip on the teat it becomes almost supernaturally strong. Instantly the lamb is much better than me at squeezing out the milk. When you're holding the lamb to the udder and you feel that unexpected power, it's as though life itself were doing the sucking . . .

19 June

We drove the sheep along the road, the paved main road outside the farm, that is. It was the long way round but we were keen – or at least the man with the dog was – to experience that scene when cars are forced to stop and wait while surrounded by a swarm of sheep. And it really was fun, everyone thought so. Besides, there was no one in a hurry on this road, not on a Sunday. The sheep couldn't care less about the cars or the asphalt surface. Every so often I have this fantasy of stopping the traffic as a radical act of resistance to everything that is destroying the natural world. Maybe the trick would be to put loads of animals on the roads.

22 June

The rams are in the big paddock up by the forest. They tend to spread out. A lot of walking is involved if you plan on counting each and every one of them. I don't have time to catch up with all of them every day.

24 June

My wife is looking through the journal. What happened to 195 in the end? she asks. I keep detailed records about the lambing in a different place. 195: two healthy lambs – without any further comment. And this was during that disastrous spring when so many of the ewes had problems. Nature is unfathomable.

25 June

I'm a vegetarian, although I eat meat from our lambs. Ethics and morals are a tricky business. I became a vegetarian when I realised how murderous the industry producing the meat in the shops was. And I'd become aware as well that animals are creatures with nervous systems and feelings. Meat is the remains of dead individuals, parts of a corpse. For a while I felt the same resistance to eating animals that I would to eating people. Then I got sheep. And children. Life isn't that simple, was what I decided at that point. I started eating meat again but only the meat that came from animals I'd taken part in killing. Working out the right moral approach is really impossible. And while some people believe it can be done, there's always something left over from all their calculations of right and wrong, a remainder you can't really define. It's like love. You can't describe exactly why you love someone, not completely. That wouldn't be love; it would be an investment decision or something like it.

26 June

I'm making more time for the rams. I'm going to count them properly, to be completely sure the number is correct. This type of grazing land may be the most authentic feature of these parts. The woods have been felled and replanted in most places; the arable land has been ploughed and drained. But these enclosed paddocks must have remained the same for many generations. There's an old oak pole with a kind of iron fitting in the middle of one of them, could it be two hundred years old? The ground is stony and uneven. Crops won't grow in it but grass does well. I step up on to a raised patch of rock and can gaze out across the plain for several kilometres. In the unlikely event I ever wanted to show off any of the surrounding area, it would be this view. I've been here for half an hour now and the rams are getting curious. They come over to me, and I'm able to count every one of them just by standing still on top of a rock.

27 June

We had rather airy-fairy theories about growing our own food, that kind of thing, when we started out. I got tired of all that after a while. I don't need any kind of explanation for why I keep sheep. That's self-evident. The fencing, the feeding . . . the whole thing. But people keep asking. So . . . why? Do you kill the animals yourself? Is that hard to do? Do you have to check on them every day? Don't you feel tied down? I try to tell them they're perfectly free to do something similar themselves, but what they mostly want is to hear me say something political. I've completely lost the ability to come out with anything political about tightening the sheep mesh or carrying a lamb over to the dry straw under the heat lamp. If I ever had it. You have to be polite though. I reply to the questions. To avoid having to justify any aspect of my life, I'd have to have a normal job, an ordinary house, ordinary friends and not do anything unexpected. And the funny thing is that's the very kind of life you ought to be questioning, because it makes you an accomplice, and a grotesquely privileged one at that, to an economic and political system that, as far as the environment is concerned, can only be seen in terms of extermination, extinction even, and as apartheid pure and simple for the poorest half of the world's population. And to cap it all some people, maybe an absolute majority even, have the cheek to set limits to how many people from the disadvantaged and poorer parts of the world can enter the country. As though we had sole rights, and naturally ordained ones at that, to our surplus.

28 June

We've got a little café on the farm now. There are some sheepskins on one wall, for sale – if the opportunity arises. I was having a coffee when someone suddenly said, that's the shepherd over there. Are they your sheep? one man asked eagerly. I've no idea why I couldn't simply say yes. An inherited reflex perhaps from generations of shepherds who know that the sheep are only yours in a superficial and far too civilised sense. Though if the skins are going to be sold, well then, maybe I should be the one to get paid. We talked about colours, patterns and woolliness, or rather he asked questions faster than I could answer; he seemed to know more about it than I did. He even came up with a price but almost immediately seemed to think it was too much.

29 June

There was a stage in my life when I thought that literature was something special, that words and phrases were
connected with and affected our musings, thoughts and
feelings. I used to think that a novel or maybe just a phrase
could conjure up an entire world, a strange one that would
suddenly seem familiar. These days I think that everything
that happens is a kind of poetry. A raven is cawing above
the sheep. That has to be saying something. Ravens can
grow old – this one might be older than me; it may have
been witness to the changes on the farm in the years we've
been keeping sheep. At some point it's bound to have
picked at part of a dead lamb. This spontaneous literature
of the natural world needs no appreciation or approval, it
belongs to no one, neither writer nor reader. It lives a life
of its own, allowing words and ideas to come and go.

30 June

I rang the county council. If the flock keeps growing, we'll go past the limit where we have to register the operation. I was told that though we've got some way to go, we still need to comply with the regulations. Right, okay. One of the crucial things is to keep the manure on a concrete slab so all the nitrogen doesn't leach into the soil. I know there's one behind the old cowshed. It'll all work out.

I've been thinking about meat again and about the time when I was a real vegetarian. The most important reason may well have been that meat-eating seemed so vulgar and greedy. Everything is constantly available in our consumer culture; there's nothing we have to do without. Meat-eating seemed to sum everything up so perfectly in that respect. Raising and then killing animals on an industrial scale to create a life of luxury and affluence is just not right. Admittedly being a vegetarian and continuing to live that same life of extravagance is pathetic, and more to the point, misguided, but at least it's doing something. I moved to the country and started keeping sheep to get away from that hedonistic nightmare. Though it hasn't entirely worked. I still live with a surfeit. If the meat in the freezer runs out all I've got to do is drive to the supermarket. The future is no doubt going to punish me for it, but I can't work out a way of escaping. What I secretly hope is that all the convenience, all that availability, when a credit card can solve all the problems of day-to-day living, will disappear. If this land, these pastures and these sheep were all I had, which was the reality for human beings in the historical past and for most of the time we've been on Earth, slaughter and meat-eating would have nothing at all to do with morality or a sustainable lifestyle. It would be a way of living and nothing more. Sun, wind, water, earth, living creatures and some fencing in an organically connected whole, with which only God himself could interfere. And not even that actually.

4 July

Like I said, I'm becoming a farmer, a grump who keeps to himself. Even so, I can't stop thinking about my place in the world. Not because I'm particularly important but because just like everyone else I'm a part of the whole. Something awful happened in one of the paddocks a few weeks ago that illustrates this phenomenon of being 'part of the whole'. A lamb died; I was forced to shoot it; my children were there. Not that I think the lamb's mother, the ewe, or any other member of the flock or my children did any grieving over it. I'm not saying that to trivialise something sad and unpleasant. I just think it's true. What happened was that one of our horses trampled the lamb so badly it had to be put down. We didn't actually see it happen but that's what must have occurred. We had let the sheep into the horses' paddock a few days before, and I noticed that the lambs were curious. They'd go up to the horses and keep nosing around until the horses got irritated and chased them off. This particular lamb would have been the least wary; it kept weaving between the legs of the horses and must have ended up under the hooves of one of them. When we got to the paddock it was lying in a little dip and couldn't get up. One of its forelegs was bent at an unnatural angle. I tried to stand it upright but it lost its balance immediately and just flopped around. The children were busy with the horses. They looked over at the lamb and me. I've got to shoot it, I said. When I came back with the rifle the children were standing round the lamb. There's nothing else we can do, so stay well back. I shot the lamb in the back of the head. The children moved in closer and saw thick blood pouring out of its mouth. Just a fact of life? I'm not sure. My daughter returned to the horses; one of my sons helped me drag the lamb away. We put it in a plastic bag. I was going to bury it the next day. Without wanting to oversimplify matters I would say this was about learning from your mistakes. Completely lost on the lamb, of course, who just ceased to exist, but there was an important lesson for the flock as a whole: Don't go too near the horses. The flock doesn't grieve for a lost individual as such; it feels a pain in part of its collective body instead. It is a wound that hurts, but one that will heal and the flock will live on, stronger and more vital.

23 July

It's dry. The grazing land is parched. The sheep are bleating. They come over when I go round the paddock, as if begging *me* for rain.

10 September

Nature in these parts isn't particularly natural. The more I learn about the woods, the pastures, the fields, the lakes and waterways and canals, the roads and buildings, the more I understand how they are all interrelated to human activity. And it has been that way for a very long time, so that determining what is natural to nature here is actually rather difficult. Beneath the layers of civilisation currently visible there are further layers of human activity from previous ages that have helped to shape the surroundings. To try to imagine a natural state of affairs in this place would be pointless, much less attempt to recreate it. I don't think there's ever been much interest in sheep here. The soil is far too fertile for such hardy, low-yield animals. Even so, I get this sense of something historical and natural when I'm following the flock of sheep; it's in the way they graze and keep moving, looking for food in the grassland and the woods. It strikes me that their behaviour, skills and character have all been developed over millennia. Though maybe time and history are irrelevant. The sheep are what they are, here and now, they're just making the best of their situation. We bought the first ones from Värmland, 300 kilometres away. Then we imported some rams, from rather far away as well. They've got nothing to do with these parts genetically or by tradition. Though they do relate to the farm in one very real way – they live off it.

11 September

I'm trying to be less dependent on praise and appreciation. I don't really know why, maybe because it's the logical thing for maintaining my mental health. When you're dependent on the judgement of others, your mood and sense of self are as fragile and unpredictable as the world around you. Only when has logic ever helped anyone? It may just be that I'm reserved and bad at sharing my feelings and experience with other people. Though a crack did open in that hard shell of mine a couple of years ago when the flock was smaller and I was less experienced. Two handymen, electricians most likely, were working on something at the back of the cowshed. They turned up early in the morning; they knew what they were supposed to do. I went over and had a chat with them after the kids had left for school. All of a sudden the sheep started bleating from the other side of the fence, fifty metres away. They recognise you, one of the men said, they didn't react to us at all this morning. I felt like I had been seen. I was touched.

12 September

If you fail to check on the sheep on a regular basis, they gradually become increasingly wild. They'll rush away from you and be difficult to manage. It's relatively easy, though, to teach them how to behave again. I think that sheep and other domesticated animals were traditionally left to take care of themselves for much of the year. It might be more rational to leave the flock alone over the summer; that would mean spending fewer working hours ... on each kilo of meat. That's how you're supposed to do the sums, I expect.

13 September

We've bought in a few sheep to add to the flock. Though we didn't really buy them, they were given to us by a city farm in Stockholm. The wretched little things have got no real future on our farm as we need the sheep we produce to be a certain size and have really nice skins. All are welcome though. One of them went off with the young ewes and escaped today. She was outside the paddock on the road running beside it. It's very rare for a single sheep to escape on its own. She was stressed out and just wanted to get back inside but couldn't find anywhere she could jump over or force a way through. We tried to corner her in part of the garden. She rushed straight past us. The second time I managed to trick her so she tried to jump right through me, which meant I could catch her in mid-flight. That feeling as you grab hold of a sheep that is almost completely out of its mind was something I'd forgotten. There was a lot of that in the first few years. The flock was on the small side, which makes the individual members scattier and less stable, and leads to a lot of escape attempts. I miss that a bit, I confess.

I carried the sheep over to the fence. It's also been a very long while since I've had to lift a sheep over the fence. She is undersized, probably the smallest member of the flock. By now almost all our sheep are cross-breeds with high-yield strains, which makes them meatier and at this point in September more or less impossible to lift over a fence. I remembered an old technique. I sort of shoved the sheep with my belly over the fence so she flew straight over and landed on all fours. That way you avoid her getting hurt. Though I really don't think sheep can hurt themselves at such low heights; in some ways they've got bodies like cats. But it feels unkind to just toss them onto the grass like a bag of potatoes. You need to have some manners at least.

16 September

Still dry. The sheep are starting to nibble away the tops of the nettles. That's how serious the situation is. But they'll survive, they're strong.

25 September

The fences are working, no problems with the water. Salt and minerals in place. I've got nothing to complain about. The sheep get up and walk away when I turn up, though one of the ewes remains lying there, as calm as an old pine tree. That's number 018; she's always been particularly sociable.

30 September

Times are changing on the farm. Perhaps that couldn't have been avoided. We've started to think of the sheep as a source of income. We're going to have even more of them and we're installing a properly accredited slaughter room. We're becoming more and more like real farmers. You've got to have an income after all; you can't just be a burden on society. On the other hand, you could build atomic weapons and make pornographic films without being a burden on society, more like an item in the government's asset column instead. Kicking pebbles and wondering about the meaning of everything, now that is highly suspect. No wonder it's hard to feel inspired.

1 October

Increasingly we've been trying to streamline the work the sheep involve and share the responsibility. I just do a quick check that they're alive, preferably from some way off. There's so much else that needs doing. Even though it was obviously a source of aggravation when they used to keep escaping, those conflicts helped to bring us closer. The constant mucking around with the sheep gave me something to base my existence on, something living and meaningful. The commercial production of meat is meaningless. A source of income but meaningless.

18 October

I have to accept that the nature of sheep-rearing has changed. Life goes on; you keep trying, groping in the dark, changing your mind. I am wandering around the little fold beside the round barn; they look over at me for a few seconds before they go back to grazing. Even some of the old ewes, who have seen me almost every day for their entire lives, appear to wonder just for a moment if I am a predator or some other kind of danger. When I started keeping sheep there was a lot of that: pausing, watching and thinking. It's much more like a job these days. That doesn't seem to be a process you can stop happening. The uncomplicated sense of being a shepherd and immersed in the life of the sheep lacks vitality now. I'm not sure why that is. It's like a lamb the ewe refuses to feed, it slowly fades away. But I still feel a closeness to the sheep and their unassuming existence. The fences, the grass, the bleating, the ruminating. The commercial production of meat may consume my time and my efforts but not my thoughts.

19 October

The man herding the sheep is having problems with 018. She's been attacking the dogs. He wants to put her down; we can't allow these genes to get passed on if we want a healthy flock. She comes over to me in the paddock. We can probably keep putting it off, I whisper.